Criminal Law for Us

Understanding Your Rights

By

Gianni The Author

ISBN: 978-0-578-71413-4

1st Edition

OTHER BOOKS WRITTEN

BY GIANNI THE AUTHOR

FICTION:

FRIENEIMES 1

FRIENEMIES 2

COMING SOON FROM GIANNI THE AUTHOR

NON-FICTION:

PRESPECTIVE IS REALITY

THE SYSTEMATIC DESTRUCTION OF OUR PEOPLE

FICTION

SWEET REVENGE 1- NOV 2021

SWEET REVENGE 2 -DEC 2021

SWEET REVENGE 3- TBA

FOR MY CHILDREN

POOKIE, JEMARI AND STINKS

EVERY BOOK I WRITE IS FOR YOU GUYS.

YOU GUYS MAY NEVER UNDERSTAND MY ACTIONS

BUT I PRAY TO THE CREATOR YOU NEVER UNDERSTAND MY PAINS.

CONTENTS

Introduction

CRIMINAL LAW FOR US is exactly what it sounds like. It is a book written for **BLACK** people to help them completely understand every aspect of criminal law while fighting a case. No matter what state you are facing legal issues in, this book will apply to your situation because it's based on your constitutional rights and the structure of our criminal injustice system. This straight to the point reference book can be used by anyone who finds themselves in a legal situation where they are facing criminal charges but like I said, it was written for my beautiful people. If you have a problem with the title and you let that detour you from this well-written wealth of knowledge, that's your choice.

As we all know, Black people, especially young black men, are incarcerated at an alarming rate. The police like to catch them young, dumb and ignorant. But ignorance of the law is no longer an excuse. After being arrested, a lot of our youth are incarcerated and represented by Court appointed attorneys. We want to believe those attorneys are fighting for our children, but we feel and see the complete opposite. Those lawyers are not fighting for our people. They are selling them out. People pretend this is a myth, but in the black community this is old news. Most Black people know exactly how corrupt the system is because in some way it has affected their family.

Mainstream media has vilified Black people for so long that society feels like it is okay to just lock us up and forget about us. They label our people killers, dealers, and gangbangers every day on the evening news city to city. In America we all know that you are guilty until proven innocent, but black criminal allegations are written and broadcasted from negative perspectives. They simply write us off and move on like it's nothing. Not caring whether it was lies or not.

Even in the hood, when a person gets locked up there is always a group of people that know nothing about the situation, but they talk about it all day (Hood News). And it is always from their perspective. We even write off our own and move on like it is nothing. I refuse to write off an entire generation of Black Kings and Queens. I do not care if they committed the crime or not. Instead of complaining on the internet about how messed up the generation is, I wrote this book to empower them. I wrote this book to give them a shot at a second chance. I wrote this book to help them understand their situation and navigate their way through our broken legal system. Millions of Black youth need this information. They need it right now so here it is. This book was written for young black generations who follow the path of the streets and have no idea how the system truly works. This book was written for every Black King and Queen locked in a county jail. It was also written for the millions of people with loved ones facing criminal allegations. I cannot make the young Kings and Queens drink, but I did provide a fully stocked well.

Many great people have been to jail and returned greater. If you're reading this from a jail cell I want you to know, **YOU ARE GREAT AND HAVE THE POWER TO RETURN GREATER**! The people on the cover of this book broke the law also. Does that mean they were wrong? Does that mean they were bad people? No. They were intelligent enough to understand their rights and bold enough to take a stand about it. They were willing to lose their physical right now freedom for the future freedoms they were entitled too. They were the type of people that didn't allow others to write them off. They chased greatness! Even from jail cells. You should do the same and can do the same. **Chase greatness!**

If you need help on a legal matter, read this book. If your son or daughter is facing criminal charges, read this book. If you just want to know about the law, read this book. It does not matter if the allegations are murder, robbery, drugs or check fraud, this book will help you understand exactly what is going on in the courtroom and behind the scenes. It is time to get educated Kings and Queens and lay your groundwork. You want to fight your case from the front-end (while it's going on) not from the back-end (inside a prison cell) after being railroaded. If you understand that, then you completely understand the purpose of this book.

The Rights That Matter

We have all heard of constitutional rights. Many people call from jail and say, "My rights are being violated". Many people tell their lawyers, "My rights are being violated". Many people even tell the judge, "My rights are being violated. Most of the time the response they get is, which one of your rights are being violated?

1. Most people have no idea which one of their rights are being violated.
2. Most people have no idea how to remedy or fix their situation legally.
3. Most mothers/family members have no idea what their loved ones are trying to explain so they ask the Court appointed attorneys only to get the run around.

This section will explain exactly which rights matter in a legal situation. What those rights are and what they mean. Regardless of which state or jurisdiction you're in, these are your rights in any criminal situation. These are the ones that matter, period. If anybody tell you different their wrong. If anyone tells you about sovereignty and how it can be applied in any U.S. courtroom their wrong. A simple check in any legal data base such as West Law or Lexis Nexus will show you case after case after case being denied. Moors Washitaw Nation, or other group that believes they will be exempted from the law in a criminal situation will be labeled a Sovereign Citizen.

What will happen if I try the Sovereign role?

The Court won't care! I cannot stress this enough. The judge or the prosecution won't care. This will be comedy to them and it makes railroading you a whole lot easier. The Court will keep proceeding with the process that was set out by the Constitution. No Treaty applies in a U.S. criminal courtroom. No Declaration applies in a U.S. criminal courtroom. Nothing in the UCC applies in a U.S. criminal courtroom. Don't get me wrong, the Kings and Queens that challenge the jurisdiction of courtrooms are strong intelligent people. They are simply applying the wrong rules to the problem. It's like bringing the rules of the NFL to the NBA! It just won't work. It's their sport

(Criminal Law) so you must learn and understand their rules to even get a grasp on the game. If you try the Sovereign role you will be railroaded throughout the entire Court process.

While facing criminal charges, the only constitutional rights that mean anything are your 4th, 5th and 6th amendment rights. The rest of them are pretty much irrelevant.

Amendment 4

Protection from Unreasonable Searches and Seizures

The right of the people to be secure in their persons, houses, papers, and effects against unreasonable searches and seizures shall not be violated, and no warrants shall issue but upon probable cause, supported by oath or affirmation, and particularly describing the place to be searched and the persons or things to be seized.

Amendment 5

Protection of Rights to Life, Liberty, and Property

No person shall be held to answer for a capital or otherwise infamous crime unless on a presentment or indictment of a grand jury, except in cases arising in the land or naval forces, or in the militia, when in actual service in time of war or public danger; nor shall any person be subject for the same offense to be twice put in jeopardy of life or limb; nor shall be compelled in any criminal case to be a witness against himself, nor be deprived of life, liberty, or property without due process of law; nor shall private property be taken for public use without just compensation.

Amendment 6

Rights of Accused Persons in Criminal Cases

In all criminal prosecutions, the accused shall enjoy the right to a speedy and public trial by an impartial jury of the state and district wherein the crime shall have been committed, which district shall have been previously ascertained by law, and to be informed of the nature and cause of the accusation; to be confronted with the witnesses against him; to have compulsory process for obtaining witnesses in his favor; and to have the assistance of counsel for his defense.

Nothing else dealing with the constitution can be applied to a criminal situation, period. Nothing else matters as far as rights. If you present any other right to any judge they will shut you down.

Breakdown of the 4th amendment

Amendment 4

Protection from Unreasonable Searches and Seizures The right of the people to be secure in their persons, houses, papers, and effects against unreasonable searches and seizures shall not be violated, and no warrants shall issue but upon probable cause, supported by oath or affirmation, and particularly describing the place to be searched and the persons or things to be seized.

What does that mean? If the cops illegally search you and find contraband, that evidence can't be used against you because it was obtained illegally. There are many different challenges to an illegal search and seizure they can be found in your state/jurisdiction case law. What is case law? I'll explain that later.

The only way to get illegal evidence tossed out is through a suppression motion also known as a **Motion to Suppress.** You should get familiar with the term **Motion to Suppress** and educate yourself on how it works because many people have won cases through suppression. No matter the case it's one of your best lines of defense.

Breakdown of the 5th amendment

Amendment 5

Protection of Rights to Life, Liberty, and Property No person shall be held to answer for a capital or otherwise infamous crime unless on a presentment or indictment of a grand jury, except in cases arising in the land or naval forces, or in the militia, when in actual service in time of war or public danger; nor shall any person be subject for the same offense to be twice put in jeopardy of life or limb; nor shall be compelled in any criminal case to be a witness against himself, nor be deprived of life, liberty, or property without due process of law; nor shall private property be taken for public use without just compensation.

What does that mean?

Most people know these rights as their Miranda rights and it basically means; **SHUT THE FUCK UP!**

You have the **RIGHT** to remain silent. Anything you say **CAN** and **WILL** be used against you in a court of law. Any good criminal defense lawyer from the late great Johnnie Cochran to a wrinkled suit public defender will tell you, "**DO NOT MAKE A STATEMENT TO THE POLICE.**"

The police are not your friends. The police are not your buddies. They don't care about the truth. They don't care about justice. Their job is to solve crimes. Are they always right? Of course not. Are they always wrong? Of course not. But they do make mistakes and cut corners, which can be exploited at trial. To do their job, the police must gather evidence. You may not know this, but words are also evidence. Your words can clean up any mistake or corner-cut they took. You will find out exactly what's going on if you're charged with a crime. No need to rush. You don't need or want the police to explain anything to you inside of a room with hidden cameras recording your every move. Also know this: **The police are allowed to lie to you while investigating a crime**. Yes, they can tell you," Kool Keith (aka KEITH AGEE) told us everything about the robbery and shooting." And it could be a flat out lie. But if that lie makes you talk it will be used in the court of law and the cop that told you the lie will admit to lying to you as an interrogation tactic. **FACTS!**

If you did the crime, but you want to get a better plea deal, **SHUT THE FUCK UP!**

If you had nothing to do with anything but you think so and so did it, **SHUT THE FUCK UP!**

If you did something with a co-defendant, **SHUT THE FUCK UP!**

Even if you don't know anything, **SHUT THE FUCK UP!**

Why should I shut the fuck up?

Because the state will use everything you say to make you a witness in the case. The state will send you subpoenas and try to get you to testify to the information you told the police. In a co-defendant situation, one person saying something can be used as probable cause to arrest the other.

What benefits will I get for talking to the police?

None. Nothing you tell the police in an interrogation room can be used for your benefit at trial. It's called a party-opponent-statement and cannot be used unless the prosecutor wants to use it.

Basically, it's their evidence not yours. Nothing you tell the police will help you be released. If they have probable cause you will be arrested. If they don't have probable cause you will be released. **Understand this**: Your words alone with zero other evidence can give police enough probable cause to arrest and charge you.

SHUT THE FUCK UP also means not discussing details of your case over a jail phone. **SHUT THE FUCK UP** also means not discussing your case with other inmates.

Why should I not discuss my case over the jail phone?

All jail phones are digitally recorded and monitored. Meaning they have endless recording capabilities and if you say anything crazy, they **CAN** and they **WILL** use it against you in a court of law. If you refused to speak to the police, (like you should've) all your jail calls will **DEFINITELY** be heavily monitored because they are trying to collect as much free information as you're willing to give up.

Why Should I not discuss my case with other inmates?

Because they can write the prosecutors office and give them intimate details about your case and become a state witness against you. Ask around, it happens all the time. They're called jailhouse snitches.

I didn't shut the fuck up! What now?

If you spoke to the police, it's not the end of the world but it makes your case much harder to win. A Motion to Suppress evidence is the main way to get statements tossed out but you'll have to research cases with situations similar circumstances surrounding the interrogation. It's the only way. There are literally thousands of cases about this issue in every state. If you spoke to the police you fucked up, so you must be active in finding a loophole out of it.

What about my bond?

As far as bond is concerned you can always have a lawyer or you yourself can appeal a high bond, but we all know that they make bonds whatever the hell they want. There are bond reduction hearings, bond commissioners and appeals. Other than that, it's the judge's decision. Don't cry about your bond, focus on your case.

What about the grand jury?

The grand jury are the people that decide whether you get indicted. In some states they also have indictment by information which is basically the same thing. The prosecution oversees both processes and they're secret. There's a saying in the criminal justice community. "The prosecutor can indict a ham sandwich." Which basically means, it's that's easy. Don't be discouraged by the charges because they must prove every one of them beyond a reasonable doubt.

What is due process of the law?

The government cannot deprive any person of life, liberty, or property without following due process of law. Both the procedures and the laws of government must be in accord with due process. The Supreme Court has refused to give an exact definition of due process and makes decisions on a case-by-case basis.

Breakdown of the 6th amendment

Amendment 6

Rights of Accused Persons in Criminal Cases in all criminal prosecutions, the accused shall enjoy the right to a speedy and public trial by an impartial jury of the state and district wherein the crime shall have been committed, which district shall have been previously ascertained by law, and to be informed of the nature and cause of the accusation; to be confronted with the witnesses against him; to have compulsory process for obtaining witnesses in his favor; and to have the assistance of counsel for his defense.

What does that mean?

Once indicted for a crime the accused has the right to a speedy trial. In most states the time frame is 90 days. The accused also has the right to a trial by Jury. This right can never be taken away and should not be waived for a bench trial. In a jury trial every single person must agree to your guilt or innocence. If the verdict is not unanimous it will be a mistrial.

Meaning they will have to drop the charges or redo trial all over. In a bench trial a single judge or three judge panel determines your guilt or innocence. Remember a lot of judges were once prosecutors, so do you really want to put your fate in their hands?

You must also be fully informed on what you're being charged with (i.e. Indictment). You also have the right to face any witness the prosecution plan on using against you. You also have the right to question and cross examine those witnesses at a public trial.

You have the right to gather your own witnesses and present them to testify on your behalf.

You also have the absolute right to the assistance of counsel. The key word is assistance. Your lawyer's job is to assist you. It's written plain as day in the U.S. Constitution. Their job is not to bully you and tell you what they're not going to do, but it happens every day across America. You'll find out how to handle those type of lawyers in the lawyer section of this book.

The 6th amendment also gives you the right to represent yourself, but it's not recommend. Only the highly intelligent should attempt to represent themselves in a criminal mater. To learn more about the rights of Self Representation please read **Faretta v. California**.

The Charges

What charges are you or your loved one facing? Is it a petty charge? Is it a serious charge? Are they incarcerated? Are they free? No matter the crime, this section will tell you how to completely understand the charges without speaking to anyone.

Regardless of the charge, all evidence collected must be given to **<u>you</u>** in what is called a **Motion of Discovery**. Notice the word you underlined because you are the one entitled to a copy, not just your attorney.

What is a Motion of Discovery?

A Motion of Discovery is all the evidence the prosecution can use against you at trial. Will they use every single piece of evidence in your **Motion of Discovery**? That's totally up to them and their trial strategy. Instead of asking jail house lawyers, CO's, or your attorney what's going on, demand your Motion of Discovery. They must give it to you. Every state/jurisdiction have different tactics to try and deny your request, but you must stay persistent until you receive your full Discovery.

Why do I want my Motion of Discovery?

You will no longer be in the dark wondering what evidence the prosecution has against you. You will now know exactly what the prosecutor has because they are not allowed to hide evidence and surprise you with it at trial. The first thing any defense lawyer does to prepare for a case is file a **Motion of Discovery**.

Once you have your full and complete **Motion of Discovery** you can then begin helping your assistant/lawyer prepare a defense for you. Without your **Motion of Discovery**, you will be completely in the dark about your case, situation, and possible sentence. **You must have a copy of your Motion of Discovery**. **NO EXCEPTIONS!** If you're incarcerated, make sure you don't leave your paperwork lying around (jail house snitches remember). When you make your bed put it between the sheet and mattress. It's that important.

What now? I have my Motion of Discovery.

Study it like your life depended on it because it does. If you don't understand what you're reading you need to figure it out because it's your case. And ignorance of the law is no excuse. The more you study it the clearer the picture will become, and you will begin to shape a reasonable defense to the allegations.

Will I need anything to help me understand the legal process and my Motion of Discovery?

Yes. You will need five books. No matter what state you're in these books will apply to any criminal situation. If it's a federal charge you will need the federal books.

1) Your state or federal- Rules of criminal procedure annotated. **(Must be annotated.)**
2) Your state or federal- Rules of evidence annotated. **(Must be annotated.)**
3) $15 Webster's dictionary.
4) $20 Black's Law Dictionary.
5) Win Your Case by Gerry Spence.

No matter the state. They all have **Rules of Criminal Procedure**, and they also all have **Rules of Evidence**. The rules will change from state to state, but they're all very similar.

How much do these books cost?

If you buy the law books brand new it will cost a few hundred in some states. A quick search of the internet will reveal used books for much cheaper. Some as low as $20. The law books do not have to be the exact year unless criminal law in your state has drastically changed in those years.

I've never heard of a Rules of Criminal Procedure book. What is it?

The Rules of Criminal Procedure is a law book that explains the criminal process from arrest to appeal. The beauty of these books are they have all the legal citing's you need to file motions and understand the legal process you're facing. The answer to most questions can be easily found in an annotated **Rules of Criminal Procedure** book.

I've never heard of the Rules of Evidence book. What is it?

The Rules of Evidence is a law book that explains how evidence can be used at trial. It also explains the process for entering that evidence. Anything entering evidence must pass through the legal loopholes of the **Rules of Evidence**. There's certain way things must be presented at trial. This book makes sure those things are being presented in the right way.

Why must those books be annotated and what does that mean?

They must be annotated because those versions provide better understanding of how the rules applies. Those versions will also provide A note, summary, or commentary on some section of a book or a statute that is intended to explain or illustrate its meaning. An annotation serves as a brief summary of the law and the facts of a case and demonstrates how a particular law enacted by Congress or a state legislature is interpreted and applied.

What is a Black's Law Dictionary? Why do I need one?

Black's Law is the most widely used law dictionary in the United States. It was founded by Henry Campbell Black (1860–1927). It is the reference of choice for terms in legal briefs and court opinions and has been cited as a secondary legal authority in many U.S. Supreme Court cases. You need this book because you'll encounter a lot of legal words you've never seen. **Black's Law Dictionary** will provide you with the definitions to these words.

What is "Win Your Case" and why do I need it?

"**Win your Case**" is a book written by Gerry Spence. This book will not only help you understand what's going on, but it will give you strategies and different ways to present your defense. If you read this book you will immediately know if your lawyer is doing his job or if he's just another slimy bastard. The author of this book is perhaps America's most renowned and successful trial lawyer. He has never lost a criminal case and has not lost a civil jury trial since 1969. Relying on the successful courtroom methods he has developed over more than half a century, Spence shows both lawyers and laypersons how you can win your case as he takes you step by step through the elements of a trial-from jury selection, the opening statement, the presentation of witnesses, their cross-examinations, and finally to the closing argument itself.

Spence teaches you how to prepare yourselves for these wars. Then he leads you through the new, cutting-edge methods he uses in discovering the story in which you form the evidence into a compelling narrative, discover the point of view of the decision maker, anticipate and answer the counterarguments, and finally conclude the case with a winning final argument.

Are you sure this is all I need?

Yes and No. Depending on your issue or situation you may need to do more research. Access to the internet or a law library combined with these books and you're ready to go. You will be prepared to fight for your freedom, which puts you ahead of 75% of people fighting criminal charges.

What is case law and why is it important?

Due to our Common Law heritage, case law has importance in the United States. Case law in this sense means the written opinions of appellate courts deciding a point of law. When judges have to make decisions on matters of law they must follow the decisions of their predecessors and superiors.

How does case law affect me?

Everybody has a boss! Including felony judges. They may appear to be mean and threatening but that is because they speak the language of case law. If you're not speaking in the language of State vs. Williams or United States vs. Jackson, they don't understand. Case law comes from the higher courts and if you find the right case law a judge must abide by it. Every judge appears to run the court room but in reality, they must follow what the higher courts say.

Who are the higher courts in my state?

No matter what state you're in, these are the ranks of the courts:

U.S. Supreme Court	Don
Federal Circuit Court	Underboss
State Supreme Court	Capo
Court of Appeals	Lt.
Your Judge	Foot Soldier

Your judge has to follow the case law of all of those above him. Every legal situation will have different case law that applies to it. That's where you find the loophole that's in every case. It's not your lawyers job to find it. It's your job and your job alone because it is a tedious process. If you find the right case law that applies to your situation, it will help free you.

Where do I find case law?

In your **Rules of Criminal Procedure** and **Rules of Evidence** books. They will be packed with many case laws. That is why you want the annotated version. Those law books will contain case laws and each one of them are about somebody's legal situation. The reason they are valuable is because most legal have already been discussed. If it's similar to your situation that's part of beginning your loophole.

Court Appointed Attorneys

I want you to take a second and think about your court appointed attorney. How many times has he or she came to see you or your loved one to discuss your case. Can you actually call them and get in touch to discuss your case? Can you write them and expect a response in a timely matter? Do you honestly even trust them?

Anyone reading this will have different responses to those questions but more than likely they won't be positive responses. The reason those responses will be negative will be because court appointed attorneys don't care about you or your legal situation. They are being paid by the state. They are not being paid by you or your loved ones so at the end of the day their loyalties lie with whomever is paying them. To make matters even worse, the state is paying them pretty shitty.

As we already covered, your 6th amendment right gives you the right to an attorney. That's doesn't mean they will be the best attorney. That doesn't mean they'll even be good. That's doesn't mean they'll care. That doesn't mean they'll dedicate every second of their work day to your case. What it means is you'll get a Court appointed attorney. Deep inside we know that these attorneys don't give a damn and that's why they always try to get you to plea out. They don't have the time or energy to focus on your case the way you need them to.

I feel like this about my lawyer. What now?

The first thing you must understand is that the lawyer works for you. As we already discussed, your 6th amendment right gives you the right to assistance of counsel. His job is to assist you. I don't care if you are 19 and he is 60, he works for you. Fuck his attitude because at the end of the day, you will be the one who ends up in prison and he will move on to the next client until his retirement days. After purchasing your books, you will be able to have intellectual conversations about different strategies and tactics with your attorney. If your lawyer doesn't respond to calls or letters concerning these tactics and strategies, then you go to his boss.

Who is my lawyer's boss?

The **State Bar Association** is your lawyers boss. All you have to do is write them a letter explaining exactly what you have asked your lawyer to do. If it is a legitimate legal request, then the bar association can and will force the lawyer to act. If the lawyer doesn't take action you can file a formal complaint against them. Remember a lawyer must have a state issued license to practice law. When you complain to the **State Bar Association** you are complaining to the people in charge of that license. You are threatening their livelihood. They will straighten up every time or just completely drop your case.

How do I get a lawyer off my case?

The first thing you must do is file a complaint with the **State Bar Association**. The second thing you must do is speak up. Don't sit back and let a punk ass attorney play with your life and freedom. No, can't get gangster with them, but you must stand up for yourself and the few rights that you do have. With a pending bar complaint against the attorney, you will have the exact definition of conflict of interest.

What is conflict of interest?

A situation in which the concerns or aims of two different parties are incompatible.

If you inform the judge about your formal complaint and stick to it, the judge will have no choice but to give you a new attorney. If you're trying to get the lawyers license stripped away how can he possibly represent you at the same time? Simply put, he can't because it's a conflict of interest.

The Prosecution

The police are the ones who throw the alley-oop. The prosecution catches the pass and attempts to slam dunk it. Every prosecutor acts like they're seeking justice but they're actually seeking convictions. If a prosecutor conviction rate isn't up to par, they'll be prosecuting low level crimes and their career will go nowhere. Understand this, the Prosecutor's Office is a political office. Everything done there is politics. They don't give a fuck about you, your case, or even the victims. Every prosecutor has a file or desk full of open cases. It's their careers they care about because they have dreams and aspirations just like everyone else. Do you honestly believe they went to college and law school because they wanted truth and justice for the common man? That education can cost anywhere between $150,000 or $250,000 depending on their school of choice.

What's the point?

The point is the prosecutor or no one in the Prosecutors' Office is your friend. You don't want to write them, have your loved ones contact them, or have anything to do with them. The only way to speak with them is through your lawyer.

Why?

Because with an open case, the Prosecutors' Office has no business speaking with you, period. It's technically against the law. It's a violation of your right to counsel. Can you imagine receiving a call or letter from the Prosecutors' Office while your case is still open? What would you do? Would you respond? No! You would hang up instantly because they are the ops.

How do I keep the prosecutor from railroading me?

The only way to keep the prosecution from railroading you is knowing the ins and outs of your case. No one should know your case better than you. If you know your case and study the books suggested there is no way the system can railroad you because you will know exactly what is going on. Prosecutors across America are railroading our people.

They've been doing it for many many years. Why? Because our people are ignorant of the law. Even if you are caught red-handed, if you know exactly what is going on, you can pump fake, drag and negotiate better plea deals. If you're in any jail facing criminal charges and you are not studying the law, you are lacking. Basically, you're saying you believe that your lawyer cares more about your freedom than you do. If you know how to read, you should be studying the law until your situation is completely over.

How much should I study the law?

The answer to that is, how much do you care about your freedom? Are card games more important than your freedom? Is Tv more important than your freedom? Do you have anything better to do to than preserving your freedom? That's how much you should study the law.

Pretrial Motions and why are they important?

A pretrial motion is basically a small battle before the war (trial). There are many different pretrial motions that can change the out come of your case. You should educate yourself on the pretrial motions needed for your situation and talk to your lawyer about filing them.

How do Pretrial motions affect my case?

If you don't research and file pretrial motions you're basically forfeiting those small battles. It's literally a fight for **YOUR** life and liberty so you shouldn't be forfeiting anything. Your job is to poke as many holes in the prosecutor's case as possible. That starts with pretrial motions. Another good thing about pretrial motions is the higher courts will review their rulings if you lose trial. If your judge ruled wrong that could possibly get you a new trial. If you want your lawyer to file a certain pretrial motion and he refuse contact the **State Bar Association**. Yes, you will be labeled as difficult but time in prison is difficult.

What pretrial motions can be filed in every state?

Motion to Suppress Evidence. Motion for Jury view. Motion for Private Investigator at State's expense.

This is one of the most important Pretrial motions that can be filed in any state and should be file.

Why Is a Private Investigator so important?

A private investigator will collect all **YOUR** evidence. A private investigator can go talk to witnesses on your behalf (legally). A private investigator is the person that collects the evidence your lawyer presents. All defense attorneys have private investigators on their payroll. A lot of people don't know how much they need a private investigator because their lawyer act like they don't need one. But why wouldn't you need a person that collects evidence for you? Of course, you do. The prosecutor has the police (who already investigated) and their own private investigators on deck. If you have a Court appointed attorney, you can easily get a private investigator because you have been ruled indigent.

The Courtroom

Courtrooms in every state and every jurisdiction were built to be intimidating and confusing. The prosecutor is spewing lie after lie like they personally know you. Armed deputies are everywhere, and the judge is talking a bunch of mumbo jumbo that you don't understand. Does this sound like the courtroom in your state? It's something called controlled chaos. It was designed to confuse and scare any person that's not there daily. If that environment is not your norm it will be very chaotic to your senses. If you calm down you'll always notice the most important person in the room, which is the person typing. **The Court Reporter** is keeping a record of everything for the higher courts. The U.S. Supreme Court said, **"A court speaks through its record."**

What does that mean?

The intimidation tactics you see and feel is not what the higher courts will see in the record.

The Court Reporter is the most important person in the room because they are preserving your plan B.

How can I use The Court Reporter in my situation?

No matter what state you're in. No matter what courtroom you're in there are a set of words to force any judge to shut up and hear you out. That phrase is: **Your Honor may I state something for the record**. When you use the phrase **"For the record"** you are no longer speaking to the judge. You are speaking to the higher courts through the record and the judge can't stop you from doing that. Remember a court speaks through its record.

Example of using the record to your benefit.

Your lawyer refuses to give you a copy of your Motion of Discovery. This is all you have to say once you're in the courtroom. **"Your Honor May I speak for the record."** No judge can stop you from speaking for the record unless you're being disruptive or just saying a bunch of bullshit. As long as you keep calm and stay cool you will be allowed to speak for the record. That's one of your absolute rights.

Once the judge gives you the floor you can't be shy. You must say "I've asked my attorney for my discovery several times and he refuse to give it to me. Once you say that on the record it will force the judge to question the attorney, which will solve your problem. Remember the small battles first then the war. If you're shy and to scared to talk for the record, you'll probably learn about your mistake in a prison law library.

The Judge

Don't take this the wrong way but the judge is nobody. Sounds crazy, right? Not so fast. America make judges seem all powerful but they're actually just referees. If you ask your lawyer, he or she will tell you that your judge is a legal referee.

How is the judge a referee?

Easy. They have a set of rules they must follow. They make sure the prosecution and defense are following the rules. They also have to settle disputes between the prosecutor and defendant.

What Rules?

The Rules of Criminal Procedure and **The Rules of Evidence**. This is exactly why you need them. It's their playbook. If you're going to trial (or every been) you understand that the jury determines guilt or innocence. Not the judge. Most felony judges have over 200 cases on the docket. That's a fact. Do you think the judge knows the details of all 200 cases on their docket? Of course not, and they don't need to know the details because they are only referees. Some of them only make calls against blatant flagrant fouls. Others are pretty good. That's how it is with refs.

What powers does a judge have?

Please don't get it confused. A judge is not completely powerless but whatever they do has to be done within a set of rules and case laws. If you know the rules and have the right case laws a judge will be easy to deal with. One of the judges most powerful weapons is something called **contempt of court.**

The only way a judge can use this power is if you're being disruptive. **NEVER BE DISRUPTIVE IN A COURTROOM**. It's the easiest way to put the ball in their court because they must restore order in the courtroom and they will.

What is Contempt of Court?

It's unappealable time in the county jail. A judge can actually put your case on hold and sentence you to 30 days 60 days 90 days, or even up to a year in some states. So never be disruptive or argumentative.

Keep calm at all times. Realize that you are the only one in the courtroom in your feelings. Everyone else in the courtroom are simply doing their job. The instant you leave the courtroom another case will come up. Another person will enter with just as much passion in their argument. Once you understand this you will understand why they're emotionless. You must be able to be the same way despite the allegations and stress of the situation.

Plea Bargain

If you plea out to a crime the judge will ask you a bunch of questions before accepting your guilty plea. When you answer those questions, you are giving the judge the right to sentence you to a variety of sentences. You are admitting to your involvement in the crime. To get the best plea bargain you must stay active in your case. You must understand all the small battles that go on before the plea offer. Those battle will weaken a prosecutor's case against you, which is why they're critical. If you do have to plea out never do it without knowing exactly how much time you're pleading to. Get your plea agreement in writing if possible.

I was offered a certain amount of time but they won't give it to me in writing?

Always remember that a court speaks through its record. If your lawyer told you that you'll only get 2 years make sure you say that on the record. The judge will ask you were you promised anything. No matter what your attorney told you to say, you make sure you cover yourself. Whatever deal he told you about spit it out. If it's a legitimate plea deal, you'll never have to hide it or act like it doesn't exist. Many of people have been told one thing and receive something different. It's your freedom so **SPEAK ON IT**.

NEVER PLEA GUILTY ALWAYS PLEA NO CONTEST IF POSSIBLE!

A no contest plea is a plea used in criminal proceedings as an alternative to a guilty or not guilty plea whereby the defendant neither disputes nor admits to doing the crime. This type of plea also known as nolo contendere, literally means "I do not wish to contend."

Why should I plea no contest?

Lawyers, prosecutors, judges, and a lot of white people know the difference between a guilty plea and a no contest plea. Guilty pleas can be used against you at later dates in civil matters. It can also be used against you later in a three strike or habitual felony offender situation. No contest means you're not admitting guilt but based on the facts of the case you don't want to contest the charges. Most no contest pleas can't be used against you at a later date. If they attempt to, you can always challenge it because you never admitted guilt.

Trial and What To Expect

Your big day is here, what now? Trial can be broken down into 7 categories.

1. **Voir dire/Jury Selection**
2. **Opening Statements**
3. **Prosecutor presents case**
4. **Defense presents case**
5. **Prosecutor rebuttal**
6. **Closing arguments**
7. **Trial objections**

If you purchase the book **"Win your Case",** you will begin to understand different tactics and strategies that can be applied to each of these categories. Every case is different so will the strategies and tactics will be different also, but the process of trial in every state is the same.

What is Voir dire?

A preliminary examination of a witness or a juror by a judge or counsel.

CRIMINAL LAW FOR US JACQUE & JYLL

What's the purpose of voir dire?

The purpose is to question and get a feel for each juror, so you can pick the best ones to decide your fate.

Is voir dire important and how does it work?

Voir dire is very important because these people are the ones who determine guilt or innocence. If you're not paying attention you could have a cop's wife on your jury. No matter what state you're in if you go to trial you will be provided with a list of potential jurors. The list will have the jurors age occupation and a little more information. A three-strike system should be used when picking jurors. If you don't like the jurors occupation give them a X. If you don't like the way they are answering questions give them a X. The third is the most important but we are taught to down play it. If you have a bad feeling about a juror or you just don't like their vibe give them three X's. Always follow your instincts during jury selection. Make sure you voice these opinions to your lawyer. You won't be able to get every person you want but having a understand of it will go a long way.

What are opening statements?

An opening statement is generally the first occasion that the trier of fact (jury or judge) has to hear from a lawyer (or self-represented defendant) in a trial, aside possibly from questioning during voir dire. The opening statement is generally constructed to serve as a "road map" for the fact-finder.

Why are Opening Statements important and how do they work?

Please read the book "**Win Your Case**" for a more detailed description. This book will also give you tactics and strategies that are very useful. The purpose of your opening statement should be to lay out every last single thing you intend to prove at trial. Opening statements are not a speech about your personal life or religious belief. Opening statements are about the facts of the case. They are very important because the prosecutor is about to call you everything but a child of God, so you must be prepared with a comeback. A lot of cases are won or lost because of Opening Statements.

Prosecution presents case

This is where the prosecutor will call their witnesses. If you've fully prepared for the battle nothing any of the prosecutor's witnesses say should surprise you. Why? Because it will be something you already read in your Motion of Discovery. Remember that the prosecutor cannot surprise or ambush you with evidence. If you've been studying your case, you'll have a well prepared cross examination for every witness.

Defense presents case

This is when your lawyer can call witnesses on your behalf. This is where your private investigator comes in at. Hopefully he's been canvassing the crime scene, talking to people who saw something different then what the police reported. Your private investigator should be questioning people who the police didn't even talk to. That's how reasonable doubt is created. Reasonable doubt is all that's needed for a not guilty verdict. The way you accomplish reasonable doubt is by presenting your own witnesses who can show your side of the coin. Most Court appointed attorneys won't have one witness come testify on your behalf. Why is that? Because you're ignorant of the law and not demanding the representation you are entitled to.

Prosecution Rebuttal

Most Black people never heard of this because their defense lawyer never subpoena their witnesses. Basically, if the defense puts on witnesses and those witnesses damage the prosecution's case the prosecutor has the right to put on witnesses to rebut your claims.

What are Closing Arguments?

A closing argument is the concluding statement of each party's counsel reiterating the important arguments for the trier of fact, (often the jury, in a court case). A closing argument occurs after the presentation of evidence.

What is the purpose of Closing Arguments?

The purpose of a closing argument is to take every point you made during trial come together. It's the bow on the perfectly wrapped present. It's your lawyer's last time to shine in front of the jury. Most juries will already have their minds made up long before Closing Arguments but there's nothing like a strong close.

For more information concerning these categories please read "**Win Your Case**". The information in that book is invaluable to anyone facing criminal charges in the U.S.

What are Trial Objections and why are they important?

Objection your Honor! I Object! We've all heard these saying on TV, but many people have no idea what they mean. An Objection is a challenge to something the prosecutor is doing. When a lawyer objects it forces the judge to pick a side concerning that objection. The judge uses case law (which are rulings from the higher court) to decide which side is right. Objections are important because the higher courts will only review things you object to unless it's a blatant miscarriage of justice.

Example:

The prosecutor enters a video into evidence but it's a video that wasn't in your Motion of Discovery. The jury use that video to convict you of the crime. When you appeal your conviction, the higher courts will say your lawyer was suppose to object (challenge) that evidence as soon as the prosecutor tried to enter it. Since your lawyer didn't object the higher courts will tell you that this is un-reviewable error.

Objections are important because they are part of your plan B. Your appeal. If you're going to trial for any crime you must remember a guilty verdict is not the end of the fight it's the beginning of your appeal.

Conclusion

If this book helped you, please tell another King or Queen about it. **EACH ONE TEACH ONE!** It's not about what you know, it's about what you pass to the next person. When you're outside of people's presence, how do the people look at you? Are you selfish? Are you money hungry? Whatever you are, if you're willing to help people and share knowledge your world will begin to transform. If this book prevented one **BLACK** King or Queen from being railroaded, I did my job.

IN LOVING MEMORY OF

TERRY FEAGIN

You provided me with knowledge, wisdom and shelter when I needed it the most. Our blueprint of farming and publishing will be fulfilled. Other than YOU and Nipsey Hussle, no other man has made such a positive impact on my life.

ZEALTH INC. is a minority-owned, publishing and social media management company. We promote positive and healthy black and brown imagery through media, both print and digital.

From the unknown artist, to unpublished author and everything in between, we dedicate ourselves to helping you see your dreams come true!

To learn more about our products and services visit us at:

EMAIL US AT: ZEALTHINC@GMAIL.COM

INSTAGRAM: @ZEALTHINC

www.ingramcontent.com/pod-product-compliance
Lightning Source LLC
Chambersburg PA
CBHW071140280326
41935CB00010B/1311

* 9 7 8 0 5 7 8 7 1 4 1 3 4 *